FIND YOUR F*CKING HAPPY

{ A Journal to Help Pave the Way for the POSITIVE Sh*t Ahead }

Monica Sweeney

CASTLE POINT BOOKS

NEW YORK

www.stmartins.com
www.castlepointbooks.com

The Castle Point Books trademark is owned by Castle Point Publishing, LLC.
Castle Point books are published and distributed by St. Martin's Press.

ISBN 978-1-250-21427-0 (trade paperback)

Design by Melissa Gerber

Images used under license by Shutterstock.com

Our books may be purchased in bulk for promotional, educational, or business
use. Please contact your local bookseller or the Macmillan Corporate and
Premium Sales Department at 1-800-221-7945, extension 5442, or by email at
MacmillanSpecialMarkets@macmillan.com.

First Edition: May 2019

10 9

THIS BOOK BELONGS TO:

_____

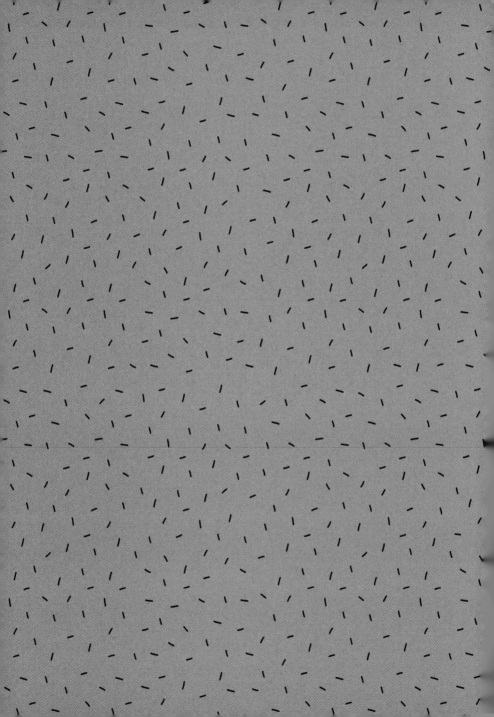

GREETINGS

Let's take a walk! To your left, you'll find a scenic view of life without the bullshit; to your right, you'll discover some lovely, soul-stirring refreshments; and straight ahead, you'll see the promise of a bright, shining tomorrow. Take a lavish dip in an effervescent bath of feel-good profanity and leave the doubters, the haters, and all your frustrations behind. Follow this journal down a picturesque path of not giving a fuck; take notice of all the special thrills, twists, and positives around you, and find your own fucking happy.

Let this book be your sparkly invitation to let go of the heavy stuff, replay the good stuff, and usher in the even better. Smash away your woes and worries like you're playing emotional Whac-a-Mole, and cash in on your wins like the champion you were born to be.

SPRINKLE YOUR WORLDVIEW
WITH A SHIT-TON OF GLEE
AND LET YOUR SOUL SHIMMER.

TICKET TO HAPPINESS

~~Happiness,~~ the Carmen Sandiego of our hearts, has the tendency to escape our grasp, jet off into the distance, and quietly plot against us. In the heart below, use a brightly colored pen or pencil to write the things that currently make you happy as a fucking clam, and, in another color, write the things you think will improve your happiness.

7

RADICAL RADIANCE

Shadows surround us. They can come in the form of self-doubt, tumultuous life events, or that odious hell-beast Sharon at work. But no matter how cold and dark those shadows can get, there is always that beam of light within you, ready to blast negativity away. When shadows start getting real, how can you shine your light into those dark corners?

_____

_____

_____

_____

_____

What reminders can you give yourself or actions can you take to get *shimmery as fuck?*

_____

_____

_____

_____

_____

"THERE ARE TWO WAYS
OF SPREADING LIGHT:
TO BE THE CANDLE
OR THE MIRROR THAT
REFLECTS IT."

—Edith Wharton

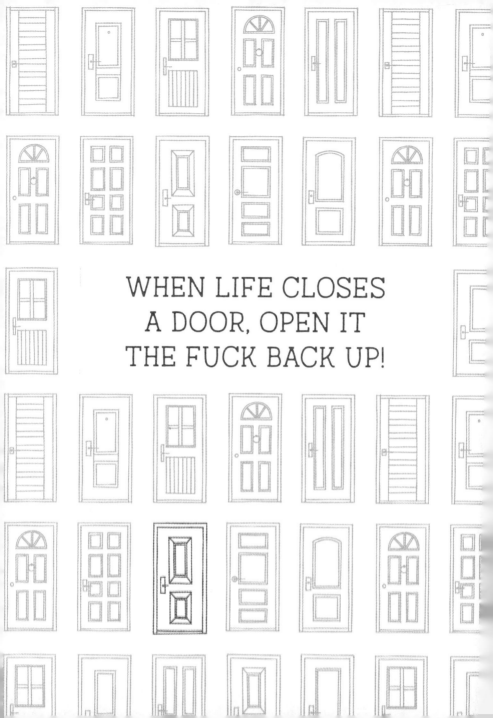

WHEN LIFE CLOSES
A DOOR, OPEN IT
THE FUCK BACK UP!

DOOR PRIZE

The wonderful thing about door technology—ancient or
modern, rusty garden gate or highfalutin pocket door—is that
doors are designed to be opened, closed, and then opened
right back up again. When a gust of wind blows your door
shut, what can you say to yourself to keep going? If the door
turns out to be fucking Alcatraz, who's to say something
behind another door isn't exactly what you need?

TRY NEW DOORS UNTIL YOU FIND
THE ONE THAT SWINGS WIDE OPEN.

"OH, WHAT A GLORIOUS DAY!"

—My Dad, regularly

SUN'S OUT, FUN'S OUT

Make your day glorious. Even if your list of worries starts tabulating the moment your eyes flutter open, or if it feels like that cartoon rain cloud won't stop spitting all over you throughout your day, take a private moment to yourself. What can you find in nature that reminds you how fucking grand our pale blue dot is? Find a nice flower, a gust of wind, or a precious meme of a fluffy little lamb to bring that awe into focus.

What's fucking glorious about your world?

_____

_____

_____

What tiny joys can you find in what's in front of you?

_____

_____

_____

_____

SISYPHEAN SILLY

No matter which mountain you choose to ascend, there will always be certain tasks, difficult people, or fuck-tons of student loan debt that keep bouldering down on you, making it feel harder and harder to climb on. While you can't just let the boulder roll down the hill and unleash its mayhem on yourself and others, you *can* make it your bitch. In the circle, draw, write, or scribble the silly, sarcastic, or ridiculous manifestations of what you want that boulder to be. Maybe deep inside, it's a sparkly geode, a jawbreaker that lost its dye, or a really gross owl pellet.

WHATEVER IT IS, LET YOURSELF FEEL MOMENTARILY UNBURDENED BY YOUR BIG, STUPID ROCK AND EMBRACE THE SPECTACULAR SILLINESS WITHIN.

"LIFE IS TOO
IMPORTANT
TO BE TAKEN
SERIOUSLY."

– Oscar Wilde

YOU'RE DOING FUCKING GREAT

No one can be a champion at everything, but you're a champion at something. Whether it's being goal-oriented, being the bright light in the room, or not going to prison for arson, you have personal strengths that you should be proud of. Below, make a list of your big strengths, your little ones, and the ones you don't always get credit for.

★ ★ ★ High Five:

_____

★ ★ Low Five:

_____

★ Fuck Off, I'm Awesome:

_____

Instead of comparing yourself to others, how can you keep those personal high fives happening?

_____

_____

_____

"WHAT DESTINY DOES NOT DO IS HOME VISITS. YOU HAVE TO GO FOR IT."

—Carlos Ruiz Zafón, *The Shadow of the Wind*

MANIFEST DESTINY, MOTHERFUCKER!

Your glittering destiny may be just around the corner or a bit farther down the road, but you won't reach it unless you get up and walk, skip, or run screaming toward it.

Where do you think your destiny lies?

_____

_____

_____

_____

How will you stake your claim to it?

_____

_____

_____

_____

"BEFORE YOU DIAGNOSE YOURSELF WITH DEPRESSION OR LOW SELF-ESTEEM, FIRST MAKE SURE THAT YOU ARE NOT, IN FACT, JUST SURROUNDED BY ASSHOLES."

—Debi Hope

CTRL + ALT + DEL

Your happiness is not up to other people, but other people can contribute to your unhappiness. When you find that a person fills you with perpetual dread or is always bringing you down, it's time for you to backspace the bad. What's preventing you from moving on from them?

_____

_____

_____

_____

How can you remove those head-asses from your life and fill the space they leave behind with positivity?*

_____

_____

_____

_____

_____

This is advice to see them less, not to be stabby.

LIST OF LAUGHS

Small reminders that life doesn't always suck can be really helpful. If you find yourself always focusing on the bad or you occasionally have the desire to break things, take a moment each day to write down something that made you break into laughter instead.

COME BACK TO THIS PAGE WHEN YOU NEED A GIGGLE!

"ONE PERSON'S
ANNOYING IS ANOTHER
PERSON'S INSPIRING
AND HEROIC."

—Leslie Knope, *Parks and Recreation*

FUCK, YEAH!

What weird little idiosyncrasies, oddities, or completely cliché
things do others roll their eyes at but make you feel great? Do
you feel inspired by the dedication of parking clerks despite
the fact that everyone gives them shit? Or maybe you get
the warm-and-fuzzies when you receive chain mail from the
relatives who still struggle with the 21st century.

*Make a list of the things that hit you right in
the ticker.*

"THE WEATHER
OUTSIDE IS WEATHER."

—Chuck, *Forgetting Sarah Marshall*

COME HELL OR HIGH WATER

Be it sunshine or storm, we all have our emotional weather patterns. Check off or write down the one that describes your internal climate, and then consider the positive aspects of each, even if they seem especially stormy. With cloudy skies and misting rain come lush forests, and with scorching heat comes margaritas.

☐ Always sunny

☐ Sunshine with a chance of scattered melancholy

☐ Mostly cloudy

☐ Tempestuous as fuck

☐ _____

Positives!

WELL, THAT ESCALATED QUICKLY

When provoked by something shitty, some people have it in them to react with that serene, Zen-like calm, where they breathe in deeply and realize that it's all going to be okay. That's so nice for those people. The rest of the population reacts by losing their shit.

Think of a scenario where you blew your fucking top and describe the fallout it caused.

_____

_____

Now, think of another one where you handled it in a manner that didn't cause mass destruction.

_____

_____

How did it feel when you realized it was okay?

_____

_____

TOTAL FUCKING NIGHTMARE: A MEMOIR

We perceive ourselves to be the protagonists of our own stories, the makers of our own dreams. Sometimes, though, we end up being our own villains. Describe a time when you were your own worst enemy.

_____

_____

_____

_____

_____

_____

_____

_____

NOW, CROSS THAT SOUL-CRUSHER OUT!

LET YOUR DREAM SELF
TELL YOUR STORY

Write your dream self—the real, fucking fantastic version of yourself who can come out victorious.

SPRITZ, SPRITZ, BITCHES

What jazzes you up the most? Whether it's an activity, a person, or a tasty fucking snack—try to capture the feeling it gives you in a few sentences.

_____

_____

_____

If you were to bottle that feeling and spritz it throughout your day, what other parts of your life would you apply it to?

_____

_____

_____

How can you spray that eau de awesome everywhere?

_____

_____

EAU DE AWESOME

LEAVE YOUR SHIT AT THE DOOR

Where is your sacred space? The kind of space—physical or mental—where you can chill the fuck out and let the worries hovering over you melt away for a moment. Whether it's a comfy corner of your home, a stress-relieving activity like yoga, or yelling into the void, make sure to treat that space with some fucking respect. Before you enter it, take a deep breath, take off the heavy emotional coat you're wearing, and go on in.

Describe your sacred space and the feelings it gives you.

_____

_____

_____

_____

How can you keep it separate from the stressful stuff?

_____

_____

_____

_____

EVERYONE IS DRUNK AND NOBODY IS LOOKING

Well, figuratively. Sometimes it seems like everyone else has their shit together. In reality, we're all at the same party. Some people are just better at hiding the fact that they're going to throw up on a rug later.

What if you found out you weren't the only one struggling?

_____

_____

_____

_____

How can you make the party fun for you?

_____

_____

_____

_____

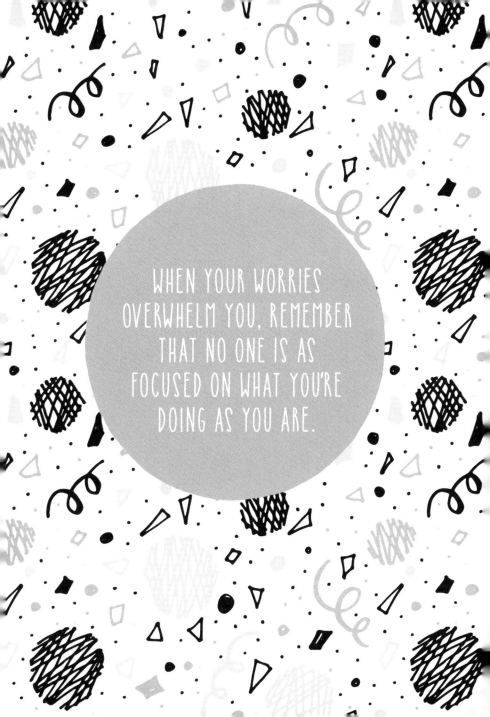

WHEN YOUR WORRIES
OVERWHELM YOU, REMEMBER
THAT NO ONE IS AS
FOCUSED ON WHAT YOU'RE
DOING AS YOU ARE.

"LET US LAY IN THE
SUN AND COUNT EVERY
BEAUTIFUL THING
WE CAN SEE."

—"In the Aeroplane Over the Sea,"
Neutral Milk Hotel

WELL, THAT'S FUCKING LOVELY

Look how many beautiful things there are in the world! On the petals of these flowers, write all the things that you can see in nature, in people, or in small details around you that are truly fucking beautiful inside or out. As the page begins to bloom with your vision of beauty, take it all in.

RETURN TO THIS MAGICAL FUCKING GARDEN WHENEVER YOU NEED A BOOST.

THE HAPPINESS THAT'S HERE

When we're surrounded by reminders of other people's happiness, it can be easy to forget the shit-ton of small and spectacular things that bring us joy. Remind yourself who and what make you happy.

 My Happy is:

_____

And this:
_____

And this:
_____

And this:
_____

And this:
_____

And this:
_____

And this:
_____

And this:
_____

And this:
_____

And this:
_____

NEW
day

OOPS, MY BAD!

Write yourself an apology note. If you've been especially hard on yourself, talked a bunch of shit, or if you're the one who keeps putting up hurdles to trip over, it's time to slow the fuck down. Say you're sorry, and then give yourself a nice, bubbly reminder of the things that are going alright.

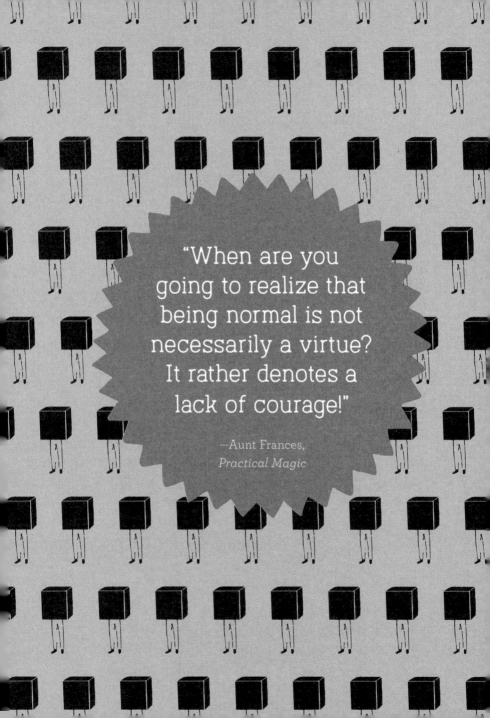

"When are you going to realize that being normal is not necessarily a virtue? It rather denotes a lack of courage!"

—Aunt Frances, *Practical Magic*

IT'S A TRAP!

Don't trap yourself in a box. Fitting in, or striving to hit all the normal milestones that you think will make you feel whole may just be your own personal version of being buried alive.

In what ways are you putting pressure on yourself to be "normal"?

_____

_____

_____

How can you embrace your quirks or your different plans in positive ways?

_____

_____

_____

KEEP THE LID OF THAT BOX OPEN, OR SPRING THE FUCK OUT OF IT.

"SERENITY NOW!"

—Frank Costanza, *Seinfeld*

FUCK-TONS OF TRANQUILITY

When you want to raise your fist and yell at the sky, maybe consider not doing that. Instead, find some tranquility in your creativity. Use your sparkly gel pens or colored pencils, and let yourself get lost in all that glorious fucking calm.

HAPPY TINGLES!

Who makes you feel the happy-tingly kind of good? Be they someone from your past or someone right in front of you, take a moment to appreciate the power of all those good feelings they inspire.

What moments stand out?

_____

_____

_____

_____

How can you pay tribute to those feelings, even if they were felt for just a moment in time?

_____

_____

_____

_____

FEELING
fucking
FANTASTIC!

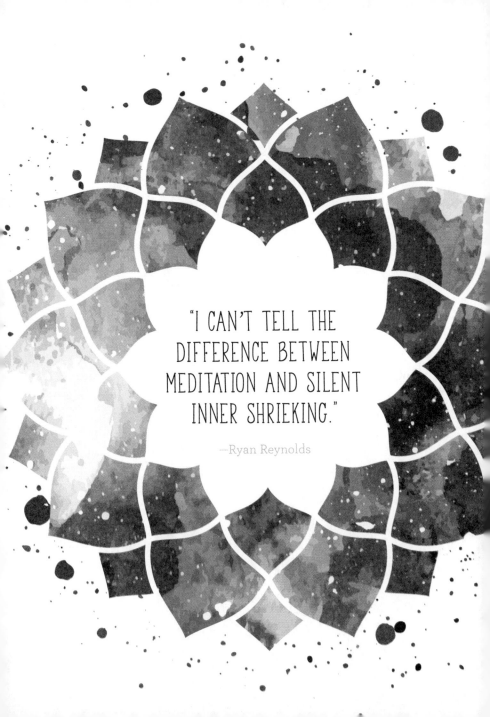

"I CAN'T TELL THE
DIFFERENCE BETWEEN
MEDITATION AND SILENT
INNER SHRIEKING."

—Ryan Reynolds

MINDFUL MELTDOWN

When everything around you starts to go fucking bonkers,
you can get caught up in the frenzy, or you can take a deep,
deep breath. Close your eyes or focus on something soothing
and methodic, like an ocean tide, the flicker of a flame, or the
swishing tail of a fucking cute puppy. What thoughts move
through your mind?

CAN YOU QUELL THAT CHAOS?

"YOU'VE ALWAYS
HAD THE POWER."

—Glinda the Good Witch

POWER UP

What makes you feel powerless? There are places that fill us with dread, people who undercut our efforts, and desserts that are just so fucking tasty that we can't resist. Write out how they make you feel.

_____

_____

_____

Now, write about what makes you feel like a spectacular badass. Can you transfer some of that verve toward the thing that makes you feel weak? If you can't right now, focus instead on that rush of energy you feel about the badass thing.

_____

_____

_____

_____

TAP YOUR RUBY SLIPPERS TOGETHER AND FEEL THAT POWER WHIRL AROUND YOU.

SLOW CLAP

The road may be long, hard, and slow, but if you can make it to your destination in one piece, who the fuck cares? What is something from your life that took way too fucking long, or that you still have ahead of you that feels like torture?

What's the worst part about this long road?

_____

_____

_____

_____

_____

What's the reward at the end of it?

_____

_____

_____

_____

_____

PICTURE IMPERFECT

No matter how stunning the photograph you see or spectacular someone else's life may seem, it is never the whole picture. (Or, it is the whole picture, but the subject sucked the soul out of the whole fucking thing by taking 27 other versions of it before slapping a filter on that one.) Paste or draw a picture of yourself in a moment of happiness or belly laughter where you didn't look perfect, but you felt pretty fucking great.

"I KNOW THIS ISN'T GONNA
END WELL, BUT THE WHOLE
MIDDLE PART IS GOING
TO BE AWESOME."

—Nick Miller, *New Girl*

EENY MEENY MINY MIDDLE

The middles of things are fucking lovely. From the middle of
a cookie to the underappreciated middle child, what comes
in the middle is often the heart and soul of something. When
it comes to life experiences, the beginnings can be nerve-
wracking and the endings can be depressing as fuck, but often
the sweet treat in the middle is worth every bit. When has the
glorious experience of the middle made up for all the rest?

_____

_____

_____

_____

Can you cherish those middles more often?

_____

_____

_____

_____

_____

HUSH, HUSH

STFU

Stop making all that racket. Devote some time to sitting in silence. Color in this page, listening only to the sounds of the colored pencil gliding against the paper, and ignore the laundry list of shit that tries to distract you.

61

"I HAVE NO TRAJECTORY.
IF I HAD A TRAJECTORY
I PROBABLY WOULD
NEVER HAVE BEEN ABLE
TO DO ALL THE FUN
THINGS I'VE DONE."

—Jameela Jamil

COZY UP WITH CHAOS

Planning is good. It leads to necessary things like city infrastructure, fire escape routes, and having all the ingredients for chocolate chip cookies in case of an emergency. But some plans—itty bitty ones that are recoverable or enormous life plans that you've counted on since childhood—can blow the fuck up.

When has a ruined plan or a blown-up plan actually worked out for you?

_____

_____

_____

What opportunities have come your way by just letting shit happen?

_____

_____

_____

LOVE YOU, MEAN IT

In the ships below, describe your favorite characteristics of your
best pals. What does their presence in your life mean to you?
How do they keep you calm when the ship is about to fucking
sink, or navigate alongside you when it's smooth sailing?

"HAPPINESS IS HAVING A LARGE, LOVING, CARING, CLOSE-KNIT FAMILY IN ANOTHER CITY."

—George Burns

FAMILY IS HARD

No two families are alike. On some days, family is our rock, and on others, we want to skip those fuckers as far out into the water as possible. Whether it's the family you were raised in or the family you've chosen, what are the qualities you love most?

_____

_____

_____

_____

Describe the cracks in the rocks, the rocks that sparkle, and the ones that are strong enough to hold up the whole fucking house.

_____

_____

_____

_____

_____

NOT TOO SHABBY

Living life by hyperbole is the worst. On one end of the spectrum are all the things that fucking-suck-and-can-rot-in-fiery-hell, and on the other are the magical-wishes-and-very-perfect parts of our lives.

NEITHER ARE ESPECIALLY REALISTIC.

Make a list of the things that are doing just fine right now.

_____

_____

_____

_____

_____

_____

_____

_____

_____

_____

_____

RAINBOWS ARE LIARS!
IN A GOOD WAY.

Rainbows, those sly motherfuckers. The result of a forlorn rainstorm and blindingly positive sunshine that just won't fuck off when it's not wanted, rainbows are the trick of light that we choose to see as beautiful.

When have you cast a rainbow on something?

_____

_____

_____

_____

What do you choose to see as beautiful?

_____

_____

_____

_____

"WELL, WELL, WELL, HOW THE TURNTABLES."

– Michael Scott, *The Office*

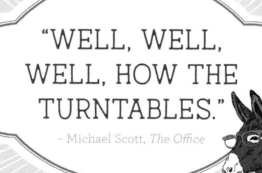

COMEUPPANCE!

When have you acted like kind of a selfish ass, only to have the situation turn on you and kick you in the teeth? In the space below, describe how it felt when the tables turned on you.

_____

_____

_____

_____

_____

Did it change how you now approach what you were doing?

_____

_____

_____

Was it something serious, or something hilarious that refuses to go off story-telling rotation amongst friends?

_____

_____

"WHEN WE ACCEPT SMALL WONDERS, WE QUALIFY OURSELVES TO IMAGINE GREAT WONDERS."

—Tom Robbins, *Jitterbug Perfume*

IT'S A WONDERFUL LIFE

What has given you a sense of awe? Of all of the many wonders of the universe, there are some that fill us with a nice little shiver of happiness and there are some that blow our fucking minds. Whether it's the smell of the ocean or the fact that there are whales alive today that were born before *Moby Dick*, these wonders give us a sense of humility and remind us that the world is pretty rad.

Little Awe	Big Awe

HELL OF A HELPER

Personal happiness isn't selfish business (unless you're a narcissist). Helping those around you—whether through volunteering, charity, or being there for a friend—goes a long way.

How has someone helped you recently?

_____

_____

_____

_____

What did their help mean to you?

_____

_____

_____

_____

Nobody likes a leech!

Make a list of things you can do in the near future to return the favor or pay it forward.

HAPPINESS ON LOOP

Some moments of happiness you can create again and again. What little bits of delight can you add again and again to each day or routine?

_____

_____

_____

Other types of bliss, like romantic relationships gone by or life before interest rates, are unlikely to come back around. Dwelling on the loss of that past happiness or trying to clone it could just turn into a science experiment gone horrifyingly wrong. What are the special parts of those good times that you can look back on with joy?

_____

_____

_____

_____

_____

_____

Spark your
own damn
happiness!

CYCLE OF GOOD.
WHEEL OF MISFORTUNE.

Hey, nice wheels. On the bad wheel below, fill out each section with the people or things that are making your life difficult. Starting from the center of each wedge, color in the amount you think this affects you. If it's only a little bit, just color in a smidge. If it's a fucking catastrophe, color in the whole damn thing. On the right side, go through the same process, but with the good stuff!

BAD   GOOD

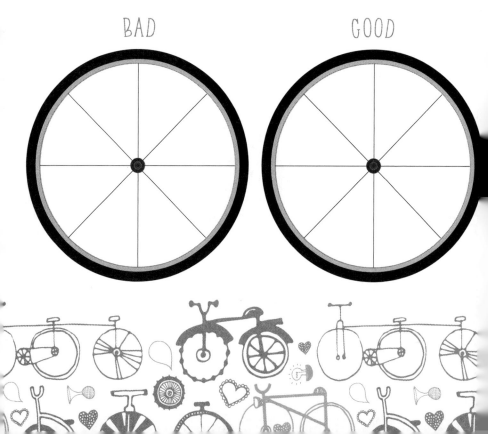

Most people will always have these two wheels, because unicycles are fucking insane. How can you make the wheels work better for you?

Vanquish THE Joyless

SPARK JOY!

You know who sucks? Fucking joyless people. The kind who look at something shimmery and just see specks of dust, or the kind who see joy in others and find a way to smother it with a pillow. In moments like those, don't let another person's lack of spark snuff yours out.

Who or what has a way of dimming your joy?

_____

_____

_____

_____

_____

How can you cast out their joylessness and keep yours shining?

_____

_____

_____

_____

_____

"PIVOT!"

—Ross Gellar, *Friends*

TURN FOR THE BETTER

Knowing when to change direction can mean the difference between getting where you want to go and slamming into the same wall over and over again. Since concussions are definitely not great, consider the ways you can recognize when to stay the course or when to pivot.

Whether it was a long-term goal or just not getting hit by a car, when has pivoting helped you?

_____

_____

_____

_____

_____

_____

_____

_____

_____

GOOD WISHES GALORE

Manifest a fuck-ton of good! In the balloons, write your good wishes for the people you love, the people you maybe just tolerate, or the people you don't know. What good wishes do you want to come their way? Is there any way you can help in the effort to make them a reality? Set them aloft here.

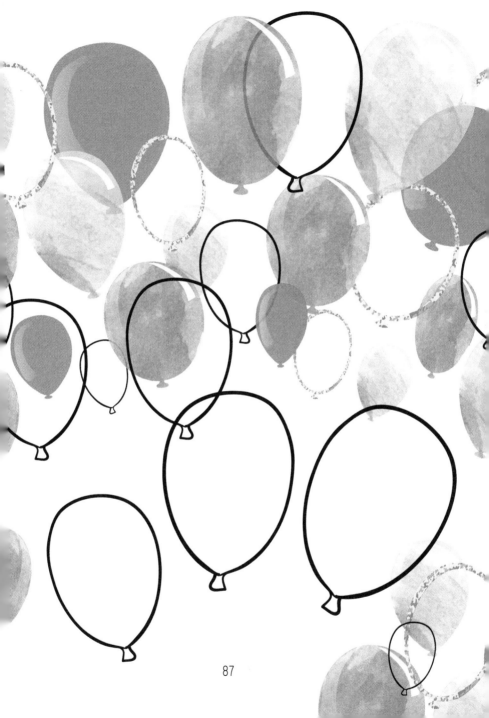

"IT IS SO WEIRD BEING MY OWN ROLE MODEL."

–Mindy Lahiri,
The Mindy Project

INSPIRATION!

Being a fucking winner doesn't come out of nowhere. In the gleaming medals below, write down the ways other people inspire you, as well as the ways you keep yourself motivated.

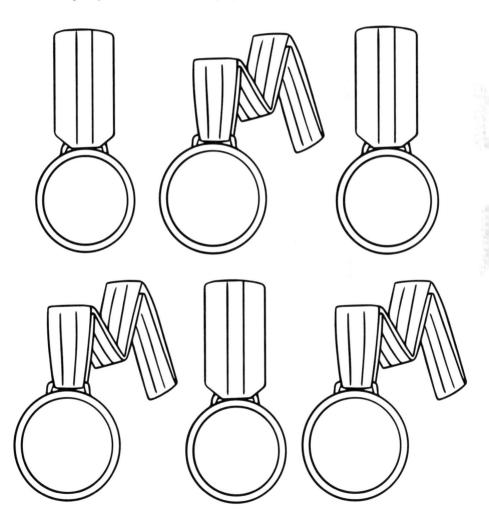

"No secrets, no longing, no desperate hoping. Just reach out and grab from a world cracked open."

–David Rakoff, *Love, Dishonor, Marry, Die, Cherish, Perish*

GET AFTER THAT SHIT

What are the goals or plans that you have been meaning to do, but just haven't gotten your shit together enough to do? Maybe it's an idea that sometimes floats across your mind, but then shiny distractions deter you from doing it. Or maybe it's something you've been telling everyone over (and over, and over, and over) again that you want to do, but you haven't put words into action. Whatever it is, write it down, think about what good it would do for you or others, and then decide how many stars it deserves on your list of priorities.

Hell, Yes, I Can…	Because…	Star Power
		☆ ☆ ☆ ☆ ☆
		☆ ☆ ☆ ☆ ☆
		☆ ☆ ☆ ☆ ☆
		☆ ☆ ☆ ☆ ☆
		☆ ☆ ☆ ☆ ☆
		☆ ☆ ☆ ☆ ☆

"THE MOST AMAZING
THINGS THAT CAN HAPPEN
TO A HUMAN BEING WILL
HAPPEN TO YOU IF YOU JUST
LOWER YOUR EXPECTATIONS."

-Phil Dunphy, *Modern Family*

MAKE TODAY FUCKING AWESOME-ISH

The best day of your life can only happen once, and you never know when that day will be. It would suck to go through each day assuming you had already had it, that it's all downhill from here, and that you may as well throw in the towel on all that happiness bullshit. Forget that noise, and let's assume your days are all on the upswing. Take small joys seriously to make each day a little bit better than if you had let them go on by. What are a few ways you can make today feel kinda-sorta the best?

_____

_____

_____

_____

_____

_____

_____

_____

_____

"Enjoy every sandwich."

–Warren Zevon

TICK-TOCK ENTANGLEMENT

Time is a fickle mistress. It moves so fast that it seems like there's never enough time to give yourself a breather or to take in the goodness of the people around you. Unless you're choosing between the red wire and the blue against a loudly beeping clock, you have time to appreciate the things around you, or to give yourself a break. Take a stroll, sip a cup of something, or talk to a friend. In the coming days, jot down what you did when you allowed yourself to step away and how it made you feel.

1 _____

2 _____

3 _____

4 _____

5 _____

6 _____

7 _____

8 _____

9 _____

10 _____

WHAT'S IT TO YOU?

Sometimes people ask for your opinion, and other times they don't. When you find yourself inclined to chime in on someone else's behavior or problems, stop and ask yourself two important questions: *Is this helpful? Am I being an asshole?* Make a list of the criticisms you have for other people or situations, and then offset that list by writing something positive and encouraging about them on the other side. Cross out the criticisms of situations that don't legitimately affect you or that you can't control, and circle the positives and consider bringing that good energy to the table. How does it feel not to care about other people's bullshit?

{ "SHE THINKS I'M TOO CRITICAL. THAT'S ANOTHER FAULT OF HERS." }

–Lucille Bluth, *Arrested Development*

This is Fucking Annoying	This is So Fucking Great!

STOP FOCUSING
ON WHAT YOU HAVEN'T
DONE YET, AND GIVE
YOURSELF SOME
FUCKING CREDIT.

LOOK HOW FAR YOU'VE COME!

The work never ends, and some seemingly short journeys end up being a long-ass pilgrimage with lots and lots of pit stops. In the middle of the diagram below, write out your big hopes. In the left-hand circle, write out all the little boosts of help or encouragement that others have given you. In the right-hand circle, write the things big and small that you're proud of doing. Look at all those amazing things!

Victory Venn Diagram!

THANK YOU, KINDLY!

Make a list of the small acts of kindness you've received from others recently.

_____

_____

_____

_____

_____

_____

_____

_____

_____

_____

IF THOSE ACTS FILLED YOU WITH
WARM FUZZIES, MADE YOU SMILE,
OR REASSURED YOU THAT HUMANITY
ISN'T COMPLETELY FUCKED,
THEN HOORAY!

Let those people know how they made you feel, and write down what that kindness means to you here.

_____

_____

_____

_____

_____

_____

_____

_____

_____

_____

_____

_____

_____

_____

_____

_____

_____

_____

_____

_____

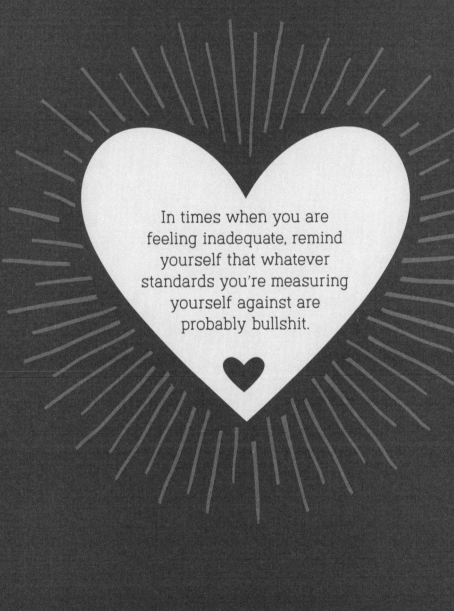

In times when you are feeling inadequate, remind yourself that whatever standards you're measuring yourself against are probably bullshit.

<3 YOU'RE ENOUGH <3

Not to be confused with *That's Enough* or *I've Had E-fucking-nough*—simply stated: You're enough. Imagine what that fullness feels like and draw or write about what it looks like to you below.

I LOVE THE SMELL OF
EXISTENTIAL DREAD
IN THE MORNING...

WAKE UP AND
SMELL THE GRATITUDE

The comforting smell of toast, the sputter of the coffee maker, or that cozy moment of bliss when you haven't yet realized you're fucking late for work—however you wake up in the morning, take a moment to breathe in some gratitude before you start your day.

What are you grateful for?

_____

_____

_____

Whether it's something big like job security or something seemingly mundane like having fucking fantastic water pressure, consider a handful of things you feel lucky to have that others may not. Let yourself mull them over for a few beats and describe why you feel what you're feeling.

_____

_____

_____

THE ANTI-RESOLUTION!

New Year's resolutions—personal betterment dressed up in sparkles and tipsy on fucking lies—rarely work for anyone. What starts as an earnest attempt at self-improvement ends up as a trash fire of despair because the goals we've set for ourselves are too high, too difficult, or too easy to mess up. Instead of setting strict goals or restrictions for yourself in the new year or in a new week, come up with 12 achievable, healthy, one-time things you're super excited about doing. Try out a new activity! Reach out to an old friend! Let yourself do something once without the pressure of a lifestyle overhaul, and if it feels good and fulfilling, see if you can keep it up.

I RESOLVE
TO HAVE
A FUCKING
LOVELY TIME

1

2

3

4

5

6

7

8

9

10

11

12

FUCK-TON OF FEARLESSNESS

Maybe your version of "fearless" is being an everyday superhero, or maybe it's just a smile plastered on your face with abject terror underneath, but let's not split hairs. What are the things that scare you?

_____

_____

_____

_____

_____

What makes you feel at ease?

_____

_____

_____

_____

Write out your favorite uplifting one-liners, song lyrics, or poems that fill you with happiness and confidence. Use them as reminders when the scaries creep in, and banish those fears away.

POW!

"BEWARE: FOR I AM FEARLESS, AND THEREFORE POWERFUL."

–Frankenstein's Monster, *Frankenstein;*
Or, the Modern Prometheus

DAYDREAM BELIEVER

Write out a recent daydream. If you didn't finish the daydream because life was rude-as-fuck and interrupted your thoughts, finish it here. Take it to an ideal place and enjoy the process of letting your thoughts unravel.

"BUT PLANT YOUR HOPE
WITH GOOD SEEDS
DON'T COVER YOURSELF WITH
THISTLE AND WEEDS."

—"Thistle & Weeds," Mumford & Sons

GOODLY GARDENING

When you plant your seeds of hope for the future, you can scatter them with abandon to yield wildflowers, or gently plant beautiful bulbs in the moonlight during solstice—or whatever biodynamic gardening magazines will tell you. But whichever method you choose, make sure the seeds you're planting aren't fucking diseased. What positive seeds do you wish to plant?

_____

Will they flourish into healthy and fruitful plants, or thorny motherfuckers?

_____

➤ Plant your garden here with all your hopes. ⬅

SHIT'S NOT FOR EVERYONE

Some social norms exist for a reason, like being a courteous neighbor and showering regularly. But others seem to have survived—nay, flourished—despite all evidence to the contrary that they're fucking awful ideas. Maybe spending all your hard-earned cash on bridesmaid duties doesn't sound like a great use of your income, or maybe partaking in the comments section of The Internets fills you with rage and regret. What are some socially encouraged activities that you've just had enough of? Make a list of the ones you'd like to quietly back away from, and imagine what good things could result if you actually do.

LLAMA
LLAMA,
fuck off
DRAMA

GRAZE ON POSITIVITY

Llamas don't give a shit. They are fluffy, majestic, and aloof to the bullshit around them. What kinds of dramatic predators surround you?

_____

_____

Instead of moving toward the drama, can you wrap yourself in that fluffy, IDGAF coat llamas wear so well?

Think of a few ways to be more like those floofers.

_____

_____

_____

_____

_____

_____

TAKE A DAMN LEAP!

It could be an emotional leap or the kind that involves lots of screaming as you ask yourself why you thought it was a good idea to go hang gliding, but taking a leap out of your comfort zone can do a world of wonders. Make a list of some of the things that you do all the time that you could switch the fuck up.

Cross those fuckers out!

Now, come up with (legal and non-threatening!) alternatives that you could try in the near future. If you do them, how did they make you feel? If you're not quite ready, what's holding you back?

_____

_____

_____

_____

_____

_____

_____

_____

_____

_____

_____

_____

"AND FROM THE MIDST
OF CHEERLESS GLOOM,
I PASSED TO BRIGHT
UNCLOUDED DAY."

—"A Little While, A Little While," Emily Brontë

CUMULONIMBUS CALAMITY

In the same way that one person can see a cute little turtle in a puffy white cloud and another can see a fucking tarantula, the clouds in our skies can be imagined in more ways than one. Take a look at the clouds outside and see what comes to mind.

_____

_____

Now, think about your personal clouds and try to re-cast them from another perspective. Are they always awful, or can they be made more cheerful? Are they perpetually rage-worthy, or are they a little bit funny?

_____

_____

_____

_____

_____

_____

SO FUCKING PRECIOUS

Do something preciously nice for yourself in the name of self-care. (The little kind of nice, not the life-crisis kind of nice.) Whether it's spraying some floral mist on your pillow so you can dream that you're spinning around in a field of flowers to your own personal *Sound of Music* scene, or taking a moment to put some cucumbers on your eyes because apparently that's still a thing, take one small action so that particular moment is just a little fucking better. Spend five minutes thinking about why it feels so fucking lovely, and then write those thoughts here.

"A NEW JOURNEY HAS BEGUN.
LET IT BE MAGICAL.
LET IT UNFOLD."

—Melody Beattie

MAKE YOUR PATH
FUCKING MAGICAL

Happiness is a big fucking word. Lest we all
succumb to the fears of never being happy with a capital H,
better to imagine the journey as a series of little happinesses
that await. Collect them on the way like little treats and enjoy
each one like it's the best fucking thing. For this last page, write
about the happiness you have, and the happiness you can give
to others. Scatter that shit like glitter as you continue on your way.

ACKNOWLEDGMENTS

Big smiles and never-ending appreciation go to Aimee Chase, Katie Jennings Campbell, Melissa Gerber, Marisa Bartlett, Jennifer Leight, Holly Schmidt, Allan Penn, and Bruce Lubin for their extra-special support and creativity. To Andy Martin, Nichole Argyres, Courtney Littler, Meryl Gross, Amelie Littell, and the whole team at St. Martin's who make this whole book-making thing so great. Lots of love and Oreos to Molly O'Grady for always speaking my language, and a very special toast to Zaida Buzan.

ABOUT THE AUTHOR

Monica Sweeney is a writer and editor.
She lives in Boston, Massachusetts.